KEEP
CALM

YOU'RE ONLY

18

Summersdale Publishers Ltd
46 West Street
Chichester
West Sussex
PO19 1RP
UK

www.summersdale.com

Printed and bound in the Czech Republic

ISBN: 978-1-84953-360-7

Substantial discounts on bulk quantities of Summersdale books are available to corporations, professional associations and other organisations. For details contact Summersdale Publishers by telephone: +44 (0) 1243 771107, fax: +44 (0) 1243 786300 or email: nicky@summersdale.com.

KEEP
CALM

YOU'RE ONLY

18

summersdale

CONTENTS

ANOTHER
YEAR
OLDER

At eighteen, everything is
possible and tomorrow
looks friendly.

Jim Bishop

The more candles,
the bigger the wish.

Anonymous

I was so surprised at being born that I didn't talk for a year and a half.

Gracie Allen

Old is like
everything else.
To make a success
of it, you've got to
start young.

Fred Astaire

Life is too short, so kiss slowly, laugh insanely, love truly and forgive quickly.

Anonymous

So far this is the
oldest I've been.

George Carlin

Born to be wild –
live to outgrow it.

Doug Horton

Every year on your
birthday, you get a
chance to start new.

Sammy Hagar

You're born
an original. Don't
die a copy.

John Mason

But age… is a
matter of feeling,
not of years.

George William Curtis

The secret of staying
young is to live honestly,
eat slowly, and lie
about your age.

Lucille Ball

The way I see it,
you should live every
day like it's your birthday.

Paris Hilton

Youth has no age.

Pablo Picasso

Life is just one
grand, sweet song,
so start the music.

Ronald Reagan

As you get older it is
harder to have heroes,
but it is sort of necessary.

Ernest Hemingway

Life is a journey,
and where your finish line is
has yet to be determined.

Anonymous

JUST
WHAT
I
ALWAYS
WANTED

Money is appropriate, and one size fits all.

William Randolph Hearst

… surprise is the greatest
gift which life can grant us.

Boris Pasternak

Birthdays are
nature's way of telling
us to eat more cake.

Jo Brand

I'm not materialistic.
I believe in presents from
the heart, like a drawing
that a child does.

Victoria Beckham

Your birthday is a special
time to celebrate the gift of
'you' to the world.

Anonymous

All the world is a birthday cake, so take a piece, but not too much.

George Harrison

Handmade presents
are scary because they
reveal that you have too
much free time.

Douglas Coupland

I wanted to buy a candle holder, but the store didn't have one. So I got a cake.

Mitch Hedberg

A well-adjusted woman is one who not only knows what she wants for her birthday, but even knows what she's going to exchange it for.

Anonymous

I only take a drink
on two occasions –
when I'm thirsty and
when I'm not.

Brendan Behan

A hug is the perfect gift,
one size fits all, and nobody
minds if you exchange it.

Anonymous

Every gift from a
friend is a wish for
your happiness.

Richard Bach

Yesterday is history,
Tomorrow is a mystery,
but Today is a gift.
That is why is it called
the present.

Eleanor Roosevelt

Celebrate the happiness
that friends are always
giving, make every day
a holiday and celebrate
just living!

Amanda Bradley

Birthday cake is the only food you can blow on and spit on and everybody rushes to get a piece.

Anonymous

GREAT
EXPECTATIONS

Accept no one's
definition of your life;
define yourself.

Harvey Fierstein

People think,
because we're young,
we aren't complex, but
that's not true.

Rihanna

Saving is a very fine
thing. Especially when
your parents have
done it for you.

Winston Churchill

The philosophy of the school room in one generation will be the philosophy of government in the next.

Abraham Lincoln

It is better to keep
your mouth closed and let
people think you are a
fool than to open it and
remove all doubt.

Mark Twain

If you obey all
the rules, you will
miss all the fun.

Katharine Hepburn

Young people want you
to be real with them.

Magic Johnson

I always say
don't make plans,
make options.

Jennifer Aniston

Life needs to be
appreciated more than
it needs to be understood.

Stuart Heller

I see what keeps
people young: work!

Ted Turner

Whoever neglects the arts when he is young has lost the past and is dead to the future.

Sophocles

Blessed are the young
for they shall inherit
the national debt.

Herbert Hoover

Fate is being kind to me.
Fate doesn't want me to be
too famous too young.

Duke Ellington

Like any young
person, I do
what I want.

Anna Kournikova

The most important thing for a young man is to establish a credit… a reputation, character.

John D. Rockefeller

When you're young you
believe it when people tell
you how good you are. And
that's the danger, you inhale.

George Clooney

SEIZE
THE
DAY

The magic of first
love is our ignorance that
it can ever end.

Benjamin Disraeli

You never really learn
to swear until you
learn to drive.

Anonymous

A man always remembers
his first love with special
tenderness, but after that he
begins to bunch them.

H. L. Mencken

Error is acceptable as long as we are young; but one must not drag it along into old age.

Johann Wolfgang von Goethe

To resist the frigidity of old age, one must combine the body, the mind, and the heart. And to keep these in parallel vigour one must exercise, study and love.

Charles-Victor de Bonstetten

It is not what a teenager knows that worries his parents. It's how he found out.

Anonymous

Exploring your sexuality is important when you're growing up.

Amanda Seyfried

When you're young,
the silliest notions
seem the greatest
achievements.

Pearl Bailey

… for the time being, I've only learned one cake recipe and how to make scrambled eggs.

Eva Herzigová

Young people discovering
their sexuality must know
they walk with a strong
tradition and that they
are not alone.

Jasmine Guy

In love, it is better
to know and be
disappointed, than to
not know and always
wonder.

Anonymous

There are no failures
– just experiences and
your reactions
to them.

Tom Krause

It is strange how often a
heart must be broken before
the years can make it wise.

Sara Teasdale

OLD
ENOUGH
TO KNOW
BETTER

If life gives you lemons, you should make lemonade.

Proverb

Before you can be
old and wise, first you
have to be young
and stupid.

Anonymous

Teenagers complain
there's nothing to do, then
stay out all night doing it.

Bob Phillips

You can't turn back the clock. But you can wind it up again.

Bonnie Prudden

Avoid hangovers, stay drunk.

Anonymous

What is a promiscuous person? It's usually someone who is getting more sex than you are.

Victor Lownes

Nothing is more
irritating than not
being invited to
a party you wouldn't
be seen dead at.

Bill Vaughan

Give me chastity
and continence,
but not yet.

St Augustine of Hippo

I'm happy to report that my inner child is still ageless.

James Broughton

The secret to eternal
youth is arrested
development.

Alice Roosevelt Longworth

It is perfectly monstrous
the way people go about
nowadays saying things
against one behind one's
back that are absolutely
and entirely true.

Oscar Wilde

A babysitter is a
teenager acting like
an adult while the
adults are out acting
like teenagers.

Anonymous

I hate to advocate drugs,
alcohol, violence or insanity
to anyone, but they've
always worked for me.

Hunter S. Thompson

Getting wasted is
only OK when you're
young enough to not
know better.

Sophia Bush

If you can't say something good about someone, sit right here by me.

Alice Roosevelt Longworth

Teenagers only have
to focus on themselves –
it's not until we get older
that we realise that other
people exist.

Jennifer Lawrence

MEASURING
MATURITY

... the last stage in
your life when you will
be happy to hear that
the phone is for you.

Fran Lebowitz
on being a teenager

At eighteen our convictions
are hills from which we look;
at forty-five they are caves
in which we hide.

F. Scott Fitzgerald

Common sense is the collection of prejudices acquired by age eighteen.

Albert Einstein

There's nothing wrong
with the younger generation
that becoming taxpayers
won't cure.

Dan Bennett

You are only young
once, but you can
be immature for
a lifetime.

John P. Grier

To me, being grown-up
meant smoking cigarettes,
drinking cocktails, and
dressing up in high heels
and glamorous outfits…

Lorna Luft

I drink
therefore I am.

W. C. Fields

I am growing up… I am losing some illusions… perhaps to acquire others.

Virginia Woolf

Those who know
they do not know
gain wisdom.
Those who
pretend they know
remain ignorant.

Lao Tzu

Growing old is mandatory; growing up is optional.

Chili Davis

Develop your eccentricities
while you are young.
That way, when you get old,
people won't think you're
going gaga.

David Ogilvy

To make mistakes is human; to stumble is commonplace; to be able to laugh at yourself is maturity.

William Arthur Ward

We grow neither better nor worse as we get old, but more like ourselves.

May Lamberton-Becker

The first sign of maturity
is the discovery that the
volume knob also turns
to the left.

Jerry M. Wright

We thought we were running away from the grown-ups, and now we are the grown-ups.

Margaret Atwood

Young man, the secret of
my success is that at an
early age I discovered
that I was not God.

Oliver Wendell Holmes, Jr.

A grown-up is a
child with layers on.

Woody Harrelson

THE
DATING
GAME

All life is an
experiment. The
more experiments
you make, the better.

Ralph Waldo Emerson

If you kiss on the first date
and it's not right, then there
will be no second date.

Jennifer Lopez

A crying baby is
the best form of
birth control.

Carole Tabron

It's difficult to decide
whether growing pains are
something teenagers have –
or are.

Anonymous

A young woman has young
claws, well sharpened.
If she has character, that is.
And if she hasn't, so much
the worse for you.

Henri Matisse

Condoms aren't completely safe. A friend of mine was wearing one and got hit by a bus.

Robert Rubin

I dated dozens of young men, had fun with all, made commitments to none.

Gene Tierney

I have no self-confidence.
When girls say yes, I tell
them to think it over.

Rodney Dangerfield

I've been in plenty of situations where someone I'm dating had more time for a console than me.

Josie Maran

Hugging closes
the door to hate.
Kissing opens the
door to love.

Tony Davis

Whenever I want a
really nice meal, I
start dating again.

Susan Healy

I married the first man I ever kissed. When I tell this to my children they just about throw up.

Barbara Bush

… the first symptom of true love in a young man is timidity, in a young woman, boldness.

Victor Hugo

I have not always
loved wisely, but
I was young.

Brigitte Bardot

Sow your wild oats on Saturday night. Then on Sunday pray for crop failure.

Anonymous

Telling a teenager the facts of life is like giving a fish a bath.

Arnold H. Glasow

My philosophy of dating is to
just fart right away.

Jenny McCarthy

**FIT
FOR
LIFE**

Don't try too hard to be young. Be who you are.

Tony Danza

Laughter is
contagious;
be a carrier.

Bobbie Siegel

If you rest, you rust.

Helen Hayes

It's amazing to me that
young people will still pick
up a cigarette.

Loni Anderson

Custom has made dancing sometimes necessary for a young man; therefore mind it while you learn it, that you may learn to do it well...

Philip Dormer Stanhope, Earl of Chesterfield

Smile!
It irritates people.

Anonymous

And, after all, what is a fashion? … a form of ugliness so intolerable that we have to alter it every six months.

Oscar Wilde

Young people
are in a condition
like permanent
intoxication, because
youth is sweet and
they are growing.

Aristotle

There is nothing
more beautiful than
believing in yourself.

Sam Kao

… you spend a large part
of your life being old,
not young.

Douglas Coupland

Try to keep your
soul young and
quivering right up
to old age.

George Sand

Always hold your head up,
but be careful to keep your
nose at a friendly level.

Max L. Forman

It's a pleasant thing
to be young and have
ten toes, and you may
lay to that.

Robert Louis Stevenson

Youth is happy because
it has the capacity to see
beauty. Anyone who keeps
the ability to see beauty
never grows old.

Franz Kafka

Life is short and messy.
Don't postpone living until
life gets neater or easier
or less frantic or more
enlightened.

Oriah Mountain Dreamer

Smile, it's the second best thing you can do with your lips.

Anonymous

THE
WORLD
IS YOUR
OYSTER

If you can imagine it,
you can achieve it;
if you can dream it,
you can become it.

William Arthur Ward

I've lived such a great, fantastic life already, but there's still so much more.

Katy Perry

Very early, I knew
that the only object in
life was to grow.

Margaret Fuller

In our dreams we
are always young.

Sarah Louise Delany

Arriving at one goal is the starting point to another.

John Dewey

Hence, courage
comes first… and
everything else
follows.

Osho

Resolve never to quit,
never to give up, no matter
what the situation.

Jack Nicklaus

Ask the young.
They know everything.

Joseph Joubert

Like all young men I
set out to be a genius,
but mercifully laughter
intervened.

Lawrence Durrell

Worse than not realising the dreams of your youth, would be to have been young and never dreamed at all.

Jean Genet

You must expect
great things of
yourself before
you can do them.

Michael Jordan

We must view young people
not as empty bottles to be
filled but as candles to be lit.

Robert H. Shaffer

The future belongs
to those who believe
in the beauty of
their dreams.

Eleanor Roosevelt

It is better to be young
in your failures than
old in your successes.

Flannery O'Connor

The young are generally
full of revolt, and are often
pretty revolting about it.

Mignon McLaughlin

Plant your own garden
and decorate your own
soul, instead of waiting
for someone to bring
you flowers.

Veronica A. Shoffstall

It's time to start
living the life
you've imagined.

Henry James

KEEP
CALM
AND
DRINK
UP

KEEP CALM AND DRINK UP

£4.99

ISBN: 978 1 84953 102 3

'*In victory, you deserve champagne; in defeat, you need it.*'

Napoleon Bonaparte

BAD ADVICE FOR GOOD PEOPLE.

Keep Calm and Carry On, a World War Two government poster, struck a chord in recent difficult times when a stiff upper lip and optimistic energy were needed again. But in the long run it's a stiff drink and flowing spirits that keep us all going.

Here's a book packed with proverbs and quotations showing the wisdom to be found at the bottom of the glass.

If you're interested in finding out more about our humour books, follow us on Twitter: @SummersdaleLOL

www.summersdale.com

KEEP
CALM
YOU'RE ONLY
18

KEEP
CALM
YOU'RE ONLY
18

KEEP
CALM
YOU'RE ONLY
18

KEEP
CALM
YOU'RE ONLY
18

KEEP
CALM
YOU'RE ONLY
18

KEEP
CALM
YOU'RE ONLY
18

KEEP CALM YOU'RE ONLY 18

KEEP CALM YOU'RE ONLY 18

KEEP CALM YOU'RE ONLY 18

KEEP CALM YOU'RE ONLY 18

KEEP CALM YOU'RE ONLY 18

KEEP CALM YOU'RE ONLY 18

KEEP CALM YOU'RE ONLY 18

KEEP CALM YOU'RE ONLY 18

KEEP CALM YOU'RE ONLY 18

KEEP CALM YOU'RE ONLY 18

KEEP CALM YOU'RE ONLY 18

KEEP CALM YOU'RE ONLY 18

KEEP CALM YOU'RE ONLY 18

KEEP CALM YOU'RE ONLY 18

KEEP CALM YOU'RE ONLY 18

KEEP CALM YOU'RE ONLY 18